THE EASY APPROACH TO FINCH CARE

by

Jennie Samuel

ISBN- 978-1467997638

Table of Contents

Part 1: Introduction to Finches

Finches constitute one of the best loved classes of birds that are kept as pets at home. From massive aviaries to cages maintained by kids, finches are kept as pets because of the birds' beautiful plumages and likable temperament and personalities.

Nearly all of the finches that are sold as domestic pets are species from the scientific family *Estrilidadae.* Many species sold in the United States originated from the tropical and subtropical regions of the world.

The easiest way to acquire finches is through pet shops and commercial aviaries. It is recommended that you find a good finch breeder/commercial aviary in your locality so that you can also consult with the experienced staff from the aviary. It is always a good thing to have actual experts that you can talk to when you need specialist knowledge about your new pets.

Are You Ready For a Finch?

Exotic birds like finches are always a mainstay of pet shops around the country. People of all ages adore these little birds because healthy finches have magnificent plumage and are also quite active, even in small cages.

But make no mistake – finches are *not like* parrots and parakeets. There are some aspects of this animal that you have to be fully prepared to deal with. If you answer a resounding "yes" to the questions below, then you are quite prepared to raise finches at home:

1. Are you prepared to raise birds that will always exhibit "wild" behavior? Finches are birds that never completely lose their wild behavior.

2. Are you willing to purchase the supplies and construct the proper housing for at least two finches? Finches fare better in societies or groups with like species. They must never be raised alone in tiny cages.

   Finches that are forced to live alone in small cages exhibit behavior similar to loneliness and may also begin showing abnormal animal behavior. Simply put, finches are *social birds* and should be given other finches as companions when kept in captivity.

3. Are you alright with the fact that finches practice behavior that may cause your home to become slightly dirty?

   For example, a finch regularly shakes off feathers and dirt. When a finch bathes, there is a big possibility that water, animal feed, feathers and litter inside the cage will end up on your floor because the finch will move around quite a bit during bathing.

It's not enough that you have *some* patience for this type of behavior. You must also be ready to *restrain yourself* from doing something harsh to the birds, like forcing their beaks into their feeding bowl or water bowl (some pet owners do this to "teach" their birds not to perform misdeeds again).

Unfortunately, like many other animals held in captivity as pets, finches *do not* associate harsh treatment with discipline. If you become physical with your finches, they will become unhappy living in your home.

4. Are you prepared to construct or purchase a large enough housing or cage for your new finches? Many people think that finches will be quite all right in a tiny cage because they are *tiny birds.*

Though it is true that the average finch is quite small, it doesn't meant that these birds don't love flying. In fact, commercial breeders will tell you that finches are happiest in outdoor enclosures that have high enough walls that provide a larger flight path.

Finches that are placed in large aviaries also tend to live longer. Pet finches have been known to live for up to ten years in captivity.

Some breeders even report that a finch that has been cared for well can live up to fifteen years in captivity. During this time, your finch would have given you several clutches of new finches already, if you created the proper conditions for breeding inside the aviary.

5. Do you have sufficient time to devote to your new finches? In addition to clean surroundings, adequate housing and proper food, captive finches also need the attention of the owner.

   Believe it or not, finches also bond with their owners – and this will not happen if you rarely visit your finches. Feeding the finches and cleaning their cage is not enough; these birds will be happier if you show them some love – that will make your finches very happy indeed.

6. If you have a family, are all your family members amenable to the idea of raising finches at home? Some people simply don't like birds because raising birds is viewed as laborious.

   Some folks also don't like birds because of asthma and allergies. All these are valid reasons *not* to keep finches at home, so make sure that you consult with your spouse and other members of your household before bringing home a pair of finches.

7. Are you prepared to take care of eggs and fledglings, should they come after you've successfully raised a pair of male and female finches in captivity?

   As we have mentioned earlier, well cared for finches can easily produce offspring in captivity.

If you are *not willing* to take care of the new fledglings, are you willing to exert a bit of time and effort to make sure that *someone else* takes in the new fledglings?

Finches & Companionship

As we have mentioned in the previous section, finches are *social birds* that require the companionship of other finches (of the same species preferably) to be completely happy in captivity.

Unlike canaries that can survive on their lonesome, finches can become *sick with loneliness*. An unhappy finch will become less active and may eat less. This can result in a myriad of health problems.

When a finch is forced to live singly in a small cage, it is possible that it will accept the companionship of other bird species just so it will have another bird to interact with.

Now, there are some instances when an aviary owner manages to introduce *different species of birds* without running into problems.

If you have a large enough aviary at home, it is possible to achieve harmony among different species of birds – but *be careful* when introducing finches to an existing community of birds.

Some finches do not like cohabiting with other species of birds. This is not bad behavior at all. We have to understand the instincts that even a third-generation captive finch still has. In the wild, birds have to travel wide distances to find adequate sources of fresh food.

Once an area with a rich food source has been found, a finch will have to defend that area from other birds – especially *bird-eating birds* that will compete for food.

The less competition in an area, the bigger the chance of survival. So when you're purchasing new finches, it would be best to check with the breeder to make sure that you can safely integrate the new finch into an existing community without causing harm to the finch itself and the other members of the bird society.

The following are finch species that *cannot* be kept with other birds (especially seed-eating species):

- *Crimson finches*

- *Bar-breasted finches*

- *Waxbill finches*

- *Melba finches*

- *Orange-winged ptylia finches*

- *Violet eared waxbill finches*

- *Diamond fire-tail finches*

- *Cutthroat finches*

- *Red headed finches*

- *Black throated finches*

- *Twin-spot finches*

If you have an existing society of finches that are of *like species,* the ratio between males and females should be *equal* to reduce competition during the mating season.

Male finches, regardless of species, can become aggressive during mating season if the aviary houses a predominantly *male* population (e.g. 10 male finches but only 6 female finches).

What about other pets like your cat and dog? In some cases, very talented pet owners are able to train their other pets to play with birds like parakeets – but this *cannot be achieved* with finches.

Finches will either shy away from other creatures or act aggressive toward other animals in your home. So the best way to keep the peace in your home is to *teach* your other pets to simply let your finches be. Dogs can easily be taught to ignore finches that are flying around the house.

Cats are a completely different story. You can't really teach cats to ignore birds, because *all cats* have feral hunting instincts.

When a finch is innocently playing in your living room and your cat comes along, it would be best to be in the same room as the two animals to avoid any problems. Finches are very delicate animals and one strong swipe or pounce from a curious, adult cat can cause wing breakage or sometimes even death.

What Are Finches Like?

For many years, finches have been kept in large aviaries because many species do well without any direct contact with their owners.

Finches have gorgeous plumage and do well in spacious, outdoor aviaries with little or no contact with other animals and humans. The *main advantage* of spacious aviaries is that the finches are free to practice nearly all of their natural behavior, including mating and the rearing of fledglings.

This is not to say that finches cannot be raised indoors in smaller cages; on the contrary, there are literally thousands of finch enthusiasts around the world who have been able to raise healthy finches in indoor enclosures and cages.

Finches that are housed indoors *can* become accustomed to human contact. Many finch owners accomplish this by *hand-feeding* their finches as frequently as possible. But before you try hand-feeding your pet, the finch *must* be well adapted to his new home. Do not try hand-feeding a newly purchased finch.

A tame finch can be held gently for short periods of time or they can be placed on T-stands or even the owner's shoulder. The birds become tame because pleasant things become firmly associated with their owners (e.g. meal time, play time, etc.).

Now, some of you may be interested in teaching a finch to copy or mimic words the way parrots do. This takes quite a bit of effort, but finches *can* be taught to speak a few words.

But do not be disappointed when your first pair of finches is not able to mimic words. Not all finch species can do this, and when you are lucky enough to find a finch that *does* mimic, it does not mean that other finches from the same group can perform the same feat.

Purchasing Finches for the First Time

Before finding this book, you may have already looked for finches at pet shops, catalogs or online stores.

And it *is* possible to order finches from websites – but we encourage *everyone* to acquire their finches from *pet shops* and *commercial breeders* or aviaries instead of buying them from pet websites and "order by mail" pet catalogs.

If you know another finch enthusiast who is known for keeping and selling avian offspring, you can also buy a pair of young finches from such an enthusiast.

We encourage everyone to visit the place where the finches are being sold. There are several benefits when you buy a finch directly from a breeder, pet shop or finch enthusiast:

1. You can see the *entire collection* of finches. You will be able to choose the exact type of finch that you want. When you order from a pet website or from an "order by mail" pet catalog, there is a chance that you might be given an animal that is not *exactly* like the one that you ordered.

   There is also a chance that you will receive a finch that is already in very poor condition. It would be cruel to ship a bird in a box through the US postal system. Birds that are transported in this manner usually become very weak from the rough travel and the mix of auto fumes they are exposed to during the trip.

2. Visiting an actual breeder or enthusiast will allow you to inspect the living conditions of all the birds. It doesn't take a veterinarian or bird expert to discover if a breeder is not treating his finches well.

   For example, if the breeder forces his finches to live in very crowded conditions with other birds, that is a sign that the breeder is not aware of the best practices in his line of work.

   Dirty cages and indoor/outdoor aviaries translate to health issues – so make sure that you check the bird for any signs of disease. Diarrhea, feather loss or balding, or anything that looks problematic should be consulted with the breeder or a veterinarian before a final purchase is made.

This way, you are a hundred percent sure that the animal you will be taking home is 100% healthy and will only need regular care from you to stay that way.

If you think a particular breeder doesn't know how to take good care of his finches, do not risk it. Say goodbye to the breeder and find another commercial breeder.

3. Finding a knowledgeable commercial finch breeder or finch enthusiast will help you establish your own network of specialists. Raising exotic pets will always be more rewarding and much easier if you have someone else to consult with regarding your finches.

The following table explores the various characteristics of healthy *and* sick finches. Let this table be your basic guide when looking for a healthy pair of finches:

Characteristic	Healthy Finch	Unhealthy Finch
Activity inside the aviary or cage	Will be on the move most of the time;	Finch appears to be fluffing up its feathers. It does

	healthy finches are frequently in flight and are constantly engaged in cleaning and preening activities.	not move much and its eyes appear to be half-closed or closed completely. If you see such a finch, you can be sure that there is something wrong with the bird.
Plumage	Smooth feathers, regular patterns are visible. No large bald patches and no irregular formations.	If the feathers near the cloaca or rear region of the finch are dirty, moist and ruffled, the finch may be suffering from parasites or other intestinal problems.
Legs	Legs have a strong, firm posture and are not bent or curved at odd	Festering wounds signal infection; the bird may also be suffering from

	angles. Scales on the legs should be nice and smooth; there should be no open or festering wounds, either.	bullying inside the aviary. A healthy finch should also have clipped nails. If the finch seems to be healthy but its nails are too long, ask the breeder to clip or file the nails for you before bringing home the finch.
Head	Eyes should be bright and alert; there should be no wounds and the top of the head should not be bald.	Balding patches on the bird's head signal illness.

Finch Species for Beginners

The following finch species are also recommended for beginning avian enthusiasts because these species are easy to take care of (compared to other species of finches):

Finch Species	Appearance
Bengalese finch	Bengalese finches usually have one solid color for the entire body, save for the head, which may have an irregular color pattern. Some Bengalese finches may also have a ring of color around its breast area.
Zebra finch	Zebra finches have a light underside and an alternating, bi-tonal striped pattern around its head, breast region and wings.
Orange-cheeked finch	Orange-cheeked finches usually come in brown and steel blue. All of them have a yellow-orange patch near the eye region.

Swee waxbill finch	Swee waxbill finches have light plumage but dark heads, with dark, slightly curved beaks.
Java sparrow finch	The Java sparrow finch is usually steel blue with a slightly pink or orange underside. The head is completely dark and is contrasted by large, white cheeks and a curved beak.
African finch	African finches come in a rainbow of colors and are usually bred so avian enthusiasts can collect all the colors they want. Characteristic of this species are the long tail feathers and small beaks (in contrast with species like the Swee waxbill finch and the Java sparrow finch).
Indian silverbill finch	The Indian silverbill finch is usually dark blue or brown with appropriate light undersides. Beaks are large, straight and slightly

	silver in color.
Spotted finch	Smaller finches with alternating spotted pattern all over its body, including its wings, cheeks and head. Only the underside is monochromatic.
White rumped finch	A stout finch with one solid color embracing the head and neck area. Half of its breast area and its entire underside are completely white. Unless bred for a colored finch collection, a white rumped finch will usually be dark brown or light brown.
Chestnut finch	Chestnut finches have three main colors: black, chestnut and light brown. A thin black ring separates the chestnut breast region from the light brown underside. The head is completely black. Wings may be a darker chestnut shade.
White headed munias	These finches have bodies

finch	that are completely brown, save for the entire head region, which is completely white.

Bringing Home a New Pair of Finches

Before purchasing finches, you should have a place ready for the birds indoors or outdoors. A large wire cage should be enough for a pair of small finches.

We will discuss the specifics of finch housing later on. In addition to housing and fresh, clean water, appropriate food should also be prepared for the finches. If your home is a few hours away from the aviary or pet shop, the finches should be given fresh food *immediately* when you arrive.

Travelling is always a bit disorienting to any kind of bird, so don't worry if your finches seem a bit dazed after the trip.

Give the birds some time to become accustomed to the new environment. Some birds become fully active after an hour's rest, while some take longer to recover. As long as you have a healthy finch in tow, you won't have to worry about transporting your new finches.

If you already have an aviary at home that is occupied by a small community of birds, *do not* mix the new finches in the aviary at once.

As with all new pets, the new finches should be quarantined in a separate cage for up to five days for routine observation. Five to seven days is usually enough time for hidden illnesses to manifest.

Once the finches are proven completely healthy during the quarantine period, it's safe to introduce them to the existing bird community or society. You would not want a pair of sick finches to make your other pet birds ill.

If this is your first time to take care of birds at home, here are some tips to get you started:

1. If you are keeping the finches indoors, ventilation is your number one priority. The cage should be situated in a place where there is adequate airflow. Otherwise, the birds could become sick from lack of proper ventilation.

2. Never buy tiny cages that were meant to be occupied by lone pet birds like canaries. Remember – finches are always instinctually seeking wider spaces to fly about.

3. All pet birds should be kept as far away as possible from heat sources like stoves. Exposure to excessive heat can be detrimental to the birds' health.

4. Finches are sensitive to sound and environment stimuli. Avoid placing finch cages near play rooms and other high-activity areas in the

house. Continuous exposure to excessive noise can cause stress to the finches.

5. Never try to touch or hold newly purchased finches. If you wish to observe them, keep your distance at first and slowly close this distance, day by day. This will allow your new birds to become accustomed to their new owner.

6. When approaching newly purchased finches, always move *slowly* and speak in low, gentle tones.

   Sudden movements and loud sounds can startle and even frighten your finches, which is counter-productive, since your main goal in the next few days is to make the birds comfortable in their new environment.

7. If your new finches are easily disturbed by activity in their immediate vicinity, it might be a good idea to drape a very thin curtain or any ordinary cloth over the cage (make sure that there is still enough exposed areas to allow proper ventilation). This thin drape will limit the stimuli until the finches become used to living in a new home.

8. Some pet shop staff will recommend a cage with a special tray for sand. It is a common misconception that sand helps the finches digest fresh food. This is not true. Sand can block the fragile digestive system of the finch and can even cause avian fatalities.

What about food? Your best guide to what food is most appropriate for your new finches is the staff from the commercial aviary, or the enthusiast who sold the finches.

If you purchased the finches from a local pet store, you might be better off consulting a veterinarian because not all pet shop staff is adequately trained when it comes to these matters.

Often, pet shop employees have inadequate knowledge because the animals are produced in commercial pet farms and are only delivered to the pet stores when they are ready to be sold as adult pets.

Now, if you wish to speed up the adaptation of the finches to a new diet, it would be wise to ask for a small amount of food from the breeder or pet shop. Mix this old food with the new bird food that you have at home. That way, the birds can immediately feed on the new bird food.

Part 2: Housing Finches

Right next to the *type* of finch that you wish to buy, the second most important consideration is *how you will house* your new finches.

It is common for some aspiring pet owners to buy the pet first *before* deciding what housing is most appropriate. We would do the opposite when dealing with finches: research and prepare the housing *before* the finches arrive, so you have fewer headaches later on.

Cage Size Does Matter

Proper housing for finches is not complicated or costly; anyone can prepare such housing provided that you follow specific guidelines when it comes to creating the perfect artificial habitat for these beautiful birds.

We must always remember that no matter how small these birds are in the wild, they fly and roam just as freely as other birds. These animals were built for *hours upon hours* of continuous flight.

So when choosing a cage, don't buy the smallest cage you can find just because the birds are only four inches long (many finches exceed this size upon full maturity).

If you do not want to spend the money for an indoor aviary (which would require a whole room and some construction), we recommend purchasing a mid-range cage that is the *largest* in its price class.

If you want to breed finches, it is imperative that you construct an outdoor or indoor aviary because finches will only engage in courtship, mating and rearing behavior if they are in a large enough area.

In fact, finches will only exhibit *most of their natural behavior* in a large enclosure. The more similar the artificial environment is to the finch's natural habitat, the better the results.

Now, if you do not have the budget for an aviary, you would be better off raising zebra finches and lady gouldian finches. These two species of finches are known to breed not only in outdoor enclosures but also in large, indoor cages. Other finches can be kept indoors, but do not expect them to breed easily.

By "breeding" we refer to the continuous process of mating, producing eggs and rearing of the fledglings. The presence of eggs is not a sure sign that the finches are actively breeding.

There are some instances when finches produce eggs but proceed to destroy or even cannibalize their own eggs. This behavior occurs when there isn't much space in the cage, or if the finches have not adapted well to their new environment.

The minimum size requirement for breeding cages for zebra finches and lady gouldian finches is 16 in. x 16 in. x 20 in. If you can construct or purchase an even larger cage, it would be even better.

Note that a 16 in. x 16 in. x 20 in. cage is sufficient for only *two finches.* If you wish to raise more than two finches at a time, you would have to invest in another cage of the same size.

The Importance of Lighting

Finches need a regular day & night cycle to survive in an artificial habitat. A day & night cycle can be accomplished through the installation of strong lighting near the indoor cage or in the outdoor aviary.

As the owner, it is your responsibility to ensure that the finches are exposed to *sufficient light* for a long enough period of time. Here's how it works:

1. The "day" cycle allows the bird to feed adequately for the entire day. In large aviaries, the "day" cycle also means that finch pairs are free to mate and care for their young.

2. The "night" cycle is reserved entirely for sleep. Finches do not really eat at night (though their behavior at night can become abnormal if the artificial "day" cycle is prolonged).

Adult finches need twelve to fourteen hours of daylight in order to feed properly and consume all their energy because in the wild, finches are known to fly vast distances looking for fresh food.

In captivity, they no longer need to do this, *however,* the birds' metabolism *is still the same* metabolism found in finches in the wild.

The finches either burn off the energy or they become sick – finches have little choice when it comes to these matters. During the winter months, the amount and *duration* of the "day" cycle has to be maintained.

Proper lighting has such a large impact on the bird's biological processes that some species of finches will not be able to develop their mature plumage without sufficient heat and light. In such instances, bright colors are not developed, and instead, the finches adopt darker plumage.

Are you keeping your finches in a cage? If your finches live in a large wire cage, you can just install a regular fluorescent light above the cage.

During nighttime (and therefore, the beginning of the finches' night cycle), you can just turn off the fluorescent light and place a light drape on the cage so the birds will not be disturbed.

In an earlier section of this book, we mentioned that new finches have to be kept in quarantine for a few days before being introduced to a large group of birds. Often, finch owners use regular cages to quarantine newly purchased finches. Other times, they use wooden "bird boxes" that only have one opening.

Though some light from an overhead fluorescent bulb can reach the interior of these bird boxes, this type of lighting is not enough to create an adequate day cycle for the bird(s) inside.

To remedy this problem, it would be best to install a light bulb *inside* the bird box to provide adequate lighting to the bird(s) inside. Mini fluorescent lights can also be used for bird boxes (bulbs in study lamps are a good choice; these bulbs provide sufficient lighting but are not too hot).

It is important that the light used is not too strong or too warm for the birds. The following table can be used when choosing the right fluorescent bulb for your own finch cage at home:

Cage Size	Wattage
Less than 40 inches in height	4 watts
At least 40 inches in height	5 to 8 watts
More than 40 inches in height	16+ watts (if the enclosure is very wide,

	multiple fluorescent bulbs must be installed to provide sufficient lighting throughout the aviary)

Notes on Installing Automatic Timers

Creating a regular day & night cycle for captive finches is easier with the help of automatic timers. Here's how it works:

1. Fluorescent lights are first installed in the aviary or above a cage.

2. Instead of plugging the lights directly into an electrical outlet, the lights are connected to an electronic timing device.

3. For the "day" cycle, the electronic timer is set to feed electricity to the fluorescent lighting for at least twelve hours. When the 12-hour mark is reached, the lights go off automatically.

4. In the morning, the electronic timer is set once again.

Some avian enthusiasts love the idea of automatic electronic timers because they no longer have to manually turn off the lights at night.

The only flaw to this system is that from "day" cycle, the finches are suddenly shrouded in complete darkness in the blink of an eye. This sudden disappearance of light is very disorienting to birds. Finches are instinctually aware that before darkness falls there is a period of *gradual darkening* or dusk.

During this short period of time, activity slows down and the finches seek their nests or resting spots in wild. Your finches should be able to do this as well. So what can you do to mimic this gradual progression from day to night?

Instead of connecting the automatic timer to the lights directly, attach a *dimming mechanism* to the automatic timer. Set the dimming mechanism to reduce the available light for thirty or forty minutes.

During this time, your finches would have already flown back to their individual resting spots in the cage or aviary and the night cycle can begin without disorienting the birds.

Interested in an Aviary?

While keeping birds in sufficiently large cages is the most common practice, constructing an aviary for your finches has its own unique advantages:

1. Aviaries provide an artificial environment that is *closest* to the type of habitat that finches seek in the wild.

2. When finches are placed in an aviary, the birds will begin to show all of their natural behavior, from mating to rearing of their young. Cages usually prevent finches from showing all of their

natural behavior. Cages also prevent many species of finches from producing avian offspring.

3. Large aviaries can adequately house large groups or societies of finches. So in the long term, constructing an aviary would be the less expensive choice for housing if you are planning to purchase more finches in the future.

Space is the biggest factor when it comes to aviaries. The minimum size of an aviary is 20 in x 20 in x 50 in. This size is adequate for a small pair of finches.

So if you are just starting out and you aren't sure if you want to buy more finches in the future, constructing an indoor/outdoor aviary with these measurements will be sufficient.

There are no hard and fast rules when it comes to determining *how many* finches should stay in a large aviary.

Some enthusiasts pack as many as twenty finches in regular, outdoor aviaries; some stick to ten to twelve finches (50% male, 50% female). If a cage or aviary looks a bit crowded when viewed from the outside, an expansion or de-congestion of the aviary is in order.

When an aviary becomes too crowded, it is possible for aggressive or overly competitive behavior to manifest in the finches.

If this happens, constructing a second aviary would be a good idea (or you can transfer one or two pairs of finches to a large cage). If you want to create your own aviary at home, here are some tips to get you started:

1. The frame of the aviary should be constructed with relatively stable material to prevent any collapses (especially if you plan on creating an outdoor aviary). Many enthusiasts make use of PVC pipes when creating aviaries. If you want a more classical look to your aviary, you can use thick, polished wood for the frames.

   If you are keeping numerous species of birds at home, you just create two or three smaller aviaries so the different species won't have to co-habit the same aviary.

   The smaller aviaries can be placed side by side. There won't be any scuffles among your bird pets because they are completely separate from each other. There won't be competition for food, water and space, too.

2. Creating an aviary need not be expensive; in fact, you can create a fairly secure aviary with the use of ordinary metal mesh. When the mesh becomes damaged, replacement and repair are also fairly easy.

3. Some of you may be interested in constructing massive outdoor aviaries that are large enough for people to walk inside and observe the finches

closely. If you have such plans, make sure to add an additional, closed-off section in the aviary.

This will ensure that no finches fly out when someone enters the aviary. You will have two doors in the outdoor aviary – one door leading into a small "receiving area" where the actual door to the aviary is located, and the actual door itself. The receiving area of the aviary should also have wire mesh so you can catch any finches that are trying to escape.

Aviary or Breeding Cages: Which is Better?

Nearly everyone likes the idea of breeding finches at home – and adult pairs *are* capable of doing this, if they get enough food, water and sufficient space to move around.

Aviaries traditionally fulfill the great role of simulating the natural environment of finches. But what happens when a large aviary becomes *congested* with other finch species and completely different bird species? You guessed it right – finches might not breed either, even if they have large space for flight.

If there is too much competition in an aviary for food (and it's difficult to monitor the feeding pattern of *every bird* in a highly populated aviary), finches might not be getting sufficient nutrition on a daily basis.

When an aviary becomes a hyper-competitive place, smaller birds may become victims of bullying. Injuries are common when there are larger, more competitive birds in the aviary.

If you have six different species of finches in one aviary, and two smaller species are not breeding properly, what can you do?

European and American finch breeders are resorting to creating *breeding cages* or *breeding flights* to remedy this problem. A breeding flight can be created in two ways:

1. You can create a closed-off section in the existing aviary and place a pair of finches inside. This closed-off section will have its own food and water troughs. With sufficient food and no competition, the pair of finches will begin to breed when the appropriate season for mating comes around.

2. If aviary modification is a bit difficult for you due to the structural design of the existing aviary, you can opt for *large breeding cages* instead. These breeding cages can be placed indoors (like some Australian finch breeders do).

   When problematic pairs of finches are separated in this manner, temperature control, light control and diet modification becomes much easier because you are operating a smaller space with *fewer birds.*

The practice of creating smaller flights of birds for breeding purposes has been met with a mix of whole-hearted support and heated criticism.

To give you a more holistic view of the matter, we are going to present *both sides* of the argument so you can make your own informed choice when the time comes.

Arguments Supporting the Practice

1. Rare birds or birds that are difficult to breed will benefit from breeding flights because they will get additional fresh food. The supply of fresh food (mealworms, etc.) is important for many species of finches.

   While some finches like the zebra finch can breed in almost any condition, other species find it impossible to breed in congested aviaries where there are six or ten other birds competing for the same food.

   The size of the bird is really one of the determining factors when it comes to dominancy inside an aviary. Inevitably, larger, more aggressive finches will get the lion's share of the fresh food.

   Smaller birds will have to wait until the larger birds are finished feeding, or they will have to fight for a good position near the feeding troughs or feeding trays. Finches are also territorial creatures; male finches can become aggressive toward other male finches during the mating season.

2. Temperature control is important *especially* if there are finch chicks in the aviary. Too often, aviaries are *under-heated* and specific areas in the aviary become too cold during nighttime.

   We must always remember that finches are *tropical* birds that require sufficient heat to survive. It is easy to supply sufficient heat in a small area and the task of installing a heating mechanism (such as a column heater) becomes less complicated because the birds are closer to the heat source in a smaller enclosure than in a regular outdoor aviary.

   Sufficient heating also means that some finches will be able to breed any time of the year, without encountering any difficulties.

   This is a great way to start breeding finches. You have a more regulated environment and fewer birds to manage every time you perform regular maintenance and monitoring of your pet finches.

3. It is generally easier to clean and maintain smaller breeding flights than a large outdoor aviary.

4. In the event that illness breaks out in a finch or mixed-bird aviary, there is a high risk of the disease being transmitted to a significant portion of the entire population in a short period of time.

When this happens, you will have to bring in a veterinarian to perform disease control in the aviary; otherwise, both the adults and the fledgling finches will suffer from mortalities.

Now, picture the same situation but with smaller flights instead of an entire aviary. Let's say there are six finches in the aviary and two pairs in two separate breeding flights.

If disease breaks out in the aviary (assuming that only one bird got sick in the beginning), only five other finches would be at risk for the same disease.

If disease broke out in *any of the separate breeding flights*, the rest of the birds in the aviary would be safe. Quarantine would be easy because the birds are already separated from one another.

5. Let's look at medical treatment now. When finches become sick, antibiotics and anti-parasite agents are often added to the drinking water.

The antibiotics are then given over a period of days at a specific strength or dosage. Imagine doing this type of treatment in an aviary with ten or twenty birds. It is *impossible* to fend off birds that are not sick – healthy birds will eventually drink the medicated water.

6. Early on we discussed the finch's need for companionship – finches should not be kept singly because these birds need to interact with other birds to live happily in an artificial environment.

   However, there are many instances when a fully packed aviary can also cause undue stress to some species of finches. And the tendency of folks who have large aviaries is to keep literally dozens of birds in one place.

   Undue stress can cause breeding problems; the presence of boisterous finch cousins in the same aviary can prevent timid breeding pairs from successfully carrying out their rearing activities.

   In some cases, smaller, more timid finches are unable to tend to their eggs (even if these eggs are completely viable and ready for hatching) because other finches in the aviary are just too active or aggressive.

Arguments Against the Practice

1. Adequate lighting and excellent temperature control will ensure that finches will survive indoors. But the big question here is: what will happen when the birds need to be reintegrated to the larger flock or finch society?

   Since the birds have adapted well to a perfectly regulated environment, it may not be able to handle actual or natural conditions outdoors.

While the birds in the outdoor aviary become "hardened" and more resilient, birds kept indoors for most of the year will become "soft" and dependent on a particular set of variables (e.g. constant heat, etc.) to survive and breed.

2. As we have mentioned repeatedly, finches are primarily *tropical birds* that require the temperature and lighting of the tropics.

   If you have a large aviary with dozens of finches, providing heating and lighting for all your birds would be quite expensive – but aesthetically, the aviary would be more enjoyable to watch than separate breeding flights.

3. After breeding, the finch chicks may not be well suited for outdoor aviaries. You may run into some problems when you start selling the young finches and the finches begin to *die* when they are placed in outdoor aviaries.

Part 3: Finch Health

What Do Finches Eat?

Like other birds, finches feed on specific items in the wild, and as the owner of these magnificent birds, it's your job to provide a balanced mix of all the edibles that finches are known to feed on.

This section of the book will tackle the specifics of a finch diet, so you should have little difficulty in acquiring the fresh and commercial foodstuffs that your birds will need to live a healthy and happy life in your home aviary or home.

Seeds Galore

Millet seed is often used by finch breeders and enthusiasts because of its wide availability. It is common practice for breeders to mix four to five types of millet. Experimenting with the mix that your own finches like is a good idea.

If you discover a favorable seed mix, waste seed will be reduced significantly and you won't have to worry about your birds not getting enough nutrition on a daily basis.

If you have the choice between buying irradiated seeds and fresh seeds, breeders recommend that you go for newer, *fresh seeds* because most species will consume fresh seeds with gusto rather than irradiated seeds. Now, once you have discovered the right combination of seeds for your finches, you can use this particular combination every month.

During the colder months of the year, it is imperative to *add* seeds to your current mix. Seeds that are rich in natural oil like hulled oats are a good choice. The finches need the extra oil in their diet to improve their resistance to cold.

Other seeds that you can use during the colder months of the year include sunflower seeds, oats, rape seeds and poppy seeds. These seeds are also added during the breeding months (early spring onward) to help jumpstart the courtship and mating of males and females in the aviary.

During the breeding season, you can also collect seeds from wild grasses in your locality. Though these seeds might not be top quality seeds in the eyes of bird mix manufacturers, finches *love* wild seeds. Don't be surprised if your finches "attack" these wild varieties more, if given the chance.

Sprouted Seeds

Sprouted seeds are also considered staple food for finches. Do not mix the dry seeds with sprouted seeds, as spoilage can occur at an accelerated rate when dry mixes are combined with moist, sprouted seeds.

Moist, sprouted seeds can only stay in the cage or aviary for a maximum of twenty-four hours. Any leftovers from yesterday's feeding must be removed immediately from the cage. During the breeding season, sprouted seeds should be provided alongside oily seeds to encourage mating behavior.

A large percentage of all finch species adore sprouted seeds. As the avian enthusiast, you can use this to your advantage. With the help of sprouted seeds, you can introduce supplements and medication to a whole group of finches with little difficulty (this applies to medication and supplements that come in powder or granular form).

Ideally, finches would ignore the slight change in the taste or consistency of the seeds when you add something to their staple food. However, there will be times that overly sensitive finches will avoid medicated sprouted seeds. If this happens, do not become frustrated.

Simply withdraw other seed mixes for the time being and keep a bowl of fresh medicated sprouted seeds in the cage or aviary. Your finches will soon visit the bowl of sprouted seeds and eat as if nothing has changed. When the medicating is over, you can reintroduce your staple dry seed mix to the flock once again.

Here is a step by step guide for creating sprouted finch seeds:

1. Depending on the amount of seeds that your finches usually consume, measure just enough fresh seeds for one or numerous feedings.

Excess sprouted seeds can be placed in a sealable container and put in the refrigerator for later use (this is also a more practical approach, since you won't have to soak seeds every day).

2. Pour the fresh seeds in a regular ice cream tub or an equivalent container. Fill this container with water.

3. Add a few drops of chlorhexidine to the water.

4. Allow the seeds to absorb moisture for one day.

5. After the initial soaking, place the seed container in a warm location in your home or outside. You need it to be at least twenty-five degrees Celsius to produce sprouted seeds.

6. When the seeds have sprouted in the water-filled container, drain the seeds.

7. If you have some powdered avian vitamins handy, it won't hurt to sprinkle a small amount on top of the sprouted seeds before serving them to your finches.

Eggs for Protein & Biscuits for Carbohydrates

You can also feed your finches a mixture of crushed biscuits and boiled chicken eggs. Biscuits for birds are available commercially; there is no need to purchase overly expensive brands because all these brands provide essentially the same thing – carbohydrates.

Boiled chicken eggs provide fat and protein. Freshly boiled eggs should be mashed thoroughly before being mixed with the biscuits.

A small amount of egg & biscuits will do every feeding. Leftover mixes should be discarded within twenty-four hours, along with unused dry seeds and sprouted seeds.

If you wish, you can also produce egg & biscuit mixes that will last for five to seven days. Just refrigerate the extra food you have for the finches, along with sprouted seeds.

Veggies & Fresh Grasses

Even seed-eaters like finches can grow fond of vegetables. To ensure that even the smallest and youngest members of your flock of finches are able to enjoy fresh cauliflowers or broccoli, it might help if you chop the fresh veggies in a food processor for a few seconds.

There are no hard and fast rules when it comes to choosing what vegetable to give your finches. If you have cucumbers at home, feed the birds cucumbers.

If you have an abundant supply of broccoli, give your finches some broccoli. But remember – the staple diet of finches will always be grains and seeds! If you live near an open field with lots of fresh grass, you can also feed these seed-bearing grasses to your finches.

To facilitate the feeding, you can create a small plastic "pocket" in the enclosure with whatever materials you have so you can just place the grass bundles there. The birds will flock to eat the seeds and after twenty-four hours you can just remove whatever is left in the "grass pocket" that you installed.

When feeding grasses and vegetables, *never* place the food directly on the floor of the cage or the aviary.

There is simply too great a risk of disease and contamination when you place the food directly on the aviary floor. No matter how much you clean an aviary, microorganisms and nasty pathogens are still lurking on the aviary floor. And remember – your aviary is *not* a natural environment. Droppings of numerous birds are concentrated in a relatively small area.

Don't like the "grass pocket" method of feeding fresh grasses to your finches? Here are some more ways to keep your fresh grasses elevated and away from the floor of the aviary:

1. You can use a spare pot (clay or plastic) as a floor-level container for grasses. Just make sure that this pot is secure and is cleaned on a daily basis. Avoid adding fresh grass to a pot full of dried or rotting grass, as this can spell disease and many other health problems.

Also, finches have a tendency to shred fresh grass when they feed, so do clean the feeding area at least once a day so the birds won't feed on random seeds on the ground.

Birds can get digestive problems *and* fungal diseases when they feed on dirty food. And when dry or fresh food mixes with droppings, the food really *is* dirty and unfit for consumption.

2. Finches are comfortable feeding while still in flight. If you like the idea of seeing finches gobbling fresh grass seeds in mid-air, you can install a looped metal wire on the ceiling of the cage or the aviary and just hang a large bunch of fresh grass on the metal loop.

   Just remember to secure the grass by tightening the loop every time you add some fresh grasses. Otherwise, the grass will just fall to the floor (and that would defeat the whole purpose of this activity).

3. A variation of method #2 exists: instead of using a looped metal wire, some avian keepers suspend a whole pot from the ceiling of the aviary.

   Of course, this method can only be used if you have a large indoor or outdoor aviary. Otherwise, the weight of pot may compromise the structural integrity of the aviary.

4. Remember those traditional mouse traps with spring-loaded clamps? You can install those mouse traps in a finch cage or aviary, too! The strong clamp can be used to securely hold the grass throughout the day. The larger the mouse trap, the bigger the bunch of fresh grasses it can hold for your beloved finches.

5. If you plan to take care of dozens of finches, a little gardening would help provide fresh grasses to all your beloved finches *for the entire year.* If you live in a location that is hot and humid, chances are grasses would be growing abundantly all year round.

Pick a particular species of grass in your locality that produces an abundant amount of seeds and transplant some live grass into a regular pot. Propagate the grass and add more pots later on.

This way, you always have fresh grass growing in your backyard and you *always* have something for the finches all year round.

This might take a bit more effort in the beginning, but no worries – your effort will be rewarded, because finches that are fed fresh grass are always happier and healthier than finches that are limited to dry or irradiated seeds. Remember our rule of thumb: the more similar the artificial environment is to the natural counterpart, the happier the finches.

Collecting Fresh Grasses

To jumpstart you grass collection duties as a new finch keeper try to find out more about the following species of grass. The following grasses are used by commercial aviary owners around the US and elsewhere because these are simply perfect for finches:

1. *Seteria palmifolia* (all Seteria grasses can be used)

2. Palm grasses

3. Pit grass

4. African feathergrass plants

5. *Pennisetum* grasses (these grasses provide food *and* are great nesting materials, too)

6. Zoo grass (common name of a popular species of grass in Australia)

7. Foxtail grasses

8. Zebra grasses

9. Tussock grasses

10.   Pampas grasses

11.   Watergrass

12.   Panic grass

13.   *Ehrharta* grasses

14.   Veldt oat plants

15.   Wintergrass

16.   Rye grass

17.   Wild canary grasses

18.   *Phalaris* plants

As Fresh As It Can Get: Live Food

Regular finches (usually, the smaller species) can fare for years on eating fresh seeds from cut grass and other dry food.

Large species, like Melba finches *won't* survive on a plant diet alone. If the breeder who sold you the finches specifically states that you have to give your finches live food, then you have to give your birds live food. There are two main ways of acquire live food for finches:

1. Collect worker termites from termite nests. If you live in a location where termite nests are plentiful, you shouldn't have too much trouble collecting enough live food for your birds on a daily basis.

2. Raise fly larvae or maggots. This is called "maggot culture" and is widely practiced because it's easy and then there is always enough live food for every finch in the aviary if the finch keeper knows how to culture larvae.

3. Purchase mealworms and fly larvae from pet shops. Note that not all pet shops have live food available, so you may have a bit of a problem in locating one that always has a fresh supply for your finches.

Culturing Fly Larvae for Finches

If you are not squeamish and you firmly believe that culturing live food is the best way to go (instead of manually collecting worker termites or buying packs of live food from pet shops), here is a step-by-step guide on how you can create your very own "larvae factory" at home:

1. For this project, you will need to construct a wooden culturing box covered with fine wire screens. The metal screen has to be fine enough to prevent mature house flies from leaving the culturing box. A regular culturing box measures 16 inches on all sides (16 in x 16 in x 16 in) and has an access panel on one side.

   The access panel should open *from the inside* so your arm will block the only exit whenever you need to clean the culturing box or add some more food for the larvae.

You should also be able to open the top of the culturing box because when "harvesting" time comes, you should have full access to the individual culturing beds/boxes inside. You will need to install light bulbs inside the culturing box to help the flies reproduce. Ten to twenty-five watt bulbs are sufficient for this purpose.

2. To start off, you need some live fly larvae (as many as you can get) from a local pet shop (if you can find one that stocks fly larvae). When people purchase fly larvae or maggots, they are usually given a *mix* of pupae and larvae. Pupae are just one step away from maturity. Larvae may be newly hatched or close to pupating.

   Place your new larval stock in a small plastic box that has been filled with calf feed and oat bran. This is the primary media and this dry mix will serve as bedding and *food* for the larvae and pupae.

   Add two more identical plastic boxes in the culturing box and fill these with the same dry mix. You can also add commercial milk powder to the dry mix, or even whey powder if you wish. Add only a small amount of these ingredients. The primary substrate is still the calf feed and the oat bran.

3. Using a regular garden sprayer, lightly spray the first box once or twice a day to add moisture to the bedding. This will help the fly larvae feed on the dry mix. In a few days (no more than five at

most), all your fly larvae will pupate. Adult flies will emerge and this is when the actual culturing begins.

You now have a small swarm of adult flies that are ready to reproduce. Keep all the plastic boxes moist to ensure that the flies have adequate bedding and food.

Alternatively, you can place a small sponge inside the culturing box and spray this sponge instead. Some finch keepers prefer this method because it requires less work.

Avoid placing water pans in culturing boxes as these pans can actually cause drowning. If you want to use shallow pans inside the culture box, you have to add bits of foam or sponge so the adult flies have something to perch on when drinking. Otherwise, the flies might drown when attempting to drink.

4. To keep the dry mix loose inside the plastic boxes, you may want to stir the material just a little every day. You won't have to do this when the larvae hatch from the eggs. You just have to prepare the substrate for the larvae.

5. After a few days, you will begin to see larvae or maggots coming out. Prepare another tray of dry mix and carefully transfer the larvae into the new tray. Place the tray in another screened box and allow the larvae to grow. If your finches

prefer pupae, just leave the larvae in the box for a longer period.

6. Twenty-four hours before feeding the larvae to your finches, sprinkle some vitamin powder on the dry mix. The larvae will ingest the vitamin powder and your finches will be able to absorb the nutrients through the live food. Mineral supplementation can also be applied through this method (e.g. calcium supplementation, etc.).

7. On the day of the feeding, you can use a blow dryer (set to low, of course) to separate the fly larvae from the loose, dry mix. Place the maggots in a small bowl and serve to your hungry finches. Congratulations, you have successfully cultured and served fly larvae to your finches!

Finch Reproduction

Breeding finches is an art that anyone can learn to master over time. This section of the book will cover the basics of finch breeding so you have an informed head start when it's time for the finches to mate and produce viable eggs.

The first thing that you have to contend with is discovering whether a finch is actually a male or a female. This process is called *sexing* and fortunately, the most common finch species can be sexed by just looking at the physical characteristics of the birds.

Boy or Girl?

The following table will help you determine the sex of your finches. Note that this table does *not* list every finch known in the trade but only provides information for visual sexing of the *most common* finch species:

Species	Males	Females
Zebra finch	Male zebra finches have a distinctive dark-orange beak that contrasts heavily with the smaller, lighter beaks of the female zebra finches. Males also have a breast bar or a solid mass of color in the chest region. Check the sides as well – the males have spotted patterns in this area.	The most reliable sign that a zebra finch is female is its breast feathers. If there is no solid bar of black in the breast region, it's a female. If you have purchased a zebra finch that is pure white, inspect the beak.

	Male zebra finches are capable of singing/warbling. Females do not.	Female zebra finches will still have a lighter orange color on their beaks.
Lady gouldian finches	Males have dark breast feathers	Females have light breast feathers. If you have lady gouldian finches that are completely white, check the head region.

Males will retain their former color during mating season. Female lady gouldian finches on the other hand, will experience darkening during the mating season.

This darkening will occur |

		regardless of the bird's plumage.
Green singer finches	Male green singer finches are noisier than female green singer finches. The plumage will also have a darker tone. The breast region of the green singer finch will be darker than the rest of its body.	Female green singer finches have a distinct ring surrounding the neck region. This ring is of a darker color than the rest of the bird's plumage.
European gold finches	Males of this species grow distinct red marks on the head region. In males, these marks can cover almost the entire face. You know you have a male when	Check the red mark on the bird's head. The intensity of the color of the feathers will be the same, but the red mark will stop as it approaches the bird's eyes.

	this coloration extends all the way to the back of the bird's head, past the eyes.	
Blue cap finches	Male blue caps have very blue head feathers (hence, the name).	Females blue caps have lighter head feathers and may have a mix of brown feathers there.
Red cheeked finches	Males have red cheek feathers.	Females do not have red cheek feathers.
Owl finches	Visual sexing is possible only during adulthood. Males have a larger chest region than the females.	Female owl finches have darker plumage and have smaller chest regions.

African red head finches	There is no size differentiation between the male African red head finches and the females of this species. Males can be identified immediately because males have reddish feathers in the head region.	Female African red head finches (ironically) don't have the same head feathers as the males.

Step One: Pairing

The pairing process in finches is similar to other bird species. Once the mating season rolls in, both males and females begin looking for potential mates.

Your role as the avian enthusiast is to make sure that all of the existing conditions in the artificial habitat are as close to *ideal* as possible. But make no mistake – a female and male finch won't mate just because another finch of the same species (and the opposite sex) is present.

In the wild, finches are continually seeking potential mates that are healthy and in top physical condition.

Active finches that exhibit strong mating behavior are also chosen over weaker members of the species that do not show much drive in pairing, and finally, mating.

Since captive finches do not have the luxury of travelling miles in search for the perfect mate, it is the finch keeper's responsibility to *make sure* that when a pair of finches are purchased, *both* the male and the female are in prime condition for pairing and mating. You wouldn't want to bring home an active, healthy male and a sickly female finch with a bald top.

If you bring home a pair of healthy finches, the chances of successful breeding rises immensely. Signs that your pair of finches are doing well together include:

- Mutual preening of feathers
- Exhibition of ornate courtship behavior
- Cooing

All you need to do at that point in time would be to prepare the *environment* for the arrival of the finch fledglings. You will have to provide a special "finch basket" during the mating season.

These small, oval baskets are made from dried strips of bamboo and are designed in a way that two birds can easily fit inside. The birds can easily enter and depart the finch basket, too.

Here's the first thing that you always have to keep in mind if you want your finches to breed: finches *don't like humans* and other animals during the mating season. Finches might be tolerant of your presence in some months, but during mating season, the *less your visibility and contact* with your pet finches, the better.

Forget about installing the finch baskets where everyone (including your dog) can see them. Finches will *not* mate and produce offspring if the basket is positioned where people and other animals are constantly passing by.

When the basket is exposed, the finches will feel that they are *vulnerable* to potential predators (including humans).

Though this might sound absurd and frustrating to some, this is how these animals view anything that can potentially threaten their survival. So instead of installing the finch baskets out in the open, try to find a spot in the aviary or cage that is a bit hidden from view.

Once the finches feel that they are hidden enough from view, they will feel *secure enough to breed.* During this time, avoid inspecting the area of the cage where the finch basket is located.

Infrequent views can be tolerated by the finches, but if you are constantly looking in the basket for finch eggs, your pair will abandon the idea of mating altogether.

Step Two: Creating a Nest

Many species of finches lay fertilized eggs just about anywhere. Finch keepers report that common varieties like zebra finches tend to randomly select spots to lay eggs.

Though this behavior may appear funny to some, it is not a good practice. Also, finches should not be allowed to lay eggs in poorly constructed nests made from dry grass (or bits of material from the cage/aviary furniture).

Since captive finches do not have access to the full range of natural materials for building strong nests, and the flimsy nests that these birds usually construct in captivity can easily disintegrate. When the nests disintegrate, you can lose a whole group of viable eggs – and you will have to wait until the pair mates again.

In rare cases where the flimsy nests survive the egg-laying and hatching period, finch fledglings usually die in the flimsy nest. To avoid this scenario, invest in finch baskets made from bamboo.

These oval baskets are not only sturdy but the wide opening mimics a natural finch nest. The mating pair can still "bring home" fragments of grass and other materials to make the nest more comfortable.

Types of Nests

The following table describes commercially available bird nests that you can find in pet shops and aviary stores:

Nest	Description
Traditional bird baskets	Full-sized, oval nests with a large opening near the top. Manufactured with strips of bamboo.
Woven bowls	Bowl-shaped nests made from strips of bamboo. Perfect for larger clutches of eggs.
Jar nests	Horizontal nests made from bamboo. Allows the birds to nestle deep inside the nest's cavity.
House nests	House-shaped bird nests with small openings. Some are multi-level structures with several entrances.
Hive-shaped nests	Resembles the hive-

	shaped nests of wild birds. Made with dried grass and can easily be suspended from the ceiling of the aviary or the top of a cage.
Pail nests	Bowl nests made from plastic with long, metal handles that can be used to suspend the nests.
Bowl nests	Nests made from plastic. These nests can be latched on to one side of the cage or aviary. Bowl nests have a very shallow cavity and may not be the best choice for finches.

Step Three: Laying Eggs

When there is successful pairing and nesting, the next phase of avian reproduction is egg-laying. This is only possible when there is harmony between the pair of finches and the conditions of the aviary or cage are just right for breeding. Don't be mistaken though, this phase of the breeding cycle does not happen overnight.

Age also plays a crucial role in the whole breeding cycle. Breeding requires female finches that are at least 9 months old. Pairing can occur earlier, but this does not mean that the female finches' body is ready for egg production. So if you paired the female at seven months, you will have to wait for an additional two to three months before the eggs start appearing.

There is usually a bit of delay between the nesting and the egg-laying. Do not be tempted to take a peek at the *inside* of the finch basket, as this will interrupt the breeding cycle. During this crucial time, it would be best to keep your distance from actively breeding pairs.

Also, don't forget to add additional live food and oily seeds to the daily diet of your finches, as the females need extra nutrition to lay eggs. Calcium supplementation is also a must, to prevent the serious health problem called "egg binding".

Egg binding occurs when a finch is unable to expel eggs because the eggs have soft, underdeveloped shells. This problem occurs when the birds experience severe malnutrition. When this happens to your own finches, you must take the birds to a veterinarian *immediately* so the bound eggs can be removed.

A boosted dose of calcium will not harden the bound eggs, but the additional supplementation can help the finch expel the offending eggs. Daily supplementation of vitamins and minerals, given through the finch's food, can help prevent this awful condition from manifesting.

An egg-bound female finch or "hen" can die from egg binding in a very short period. What does an egg-bound finch look like? In addition to immobility (the female will be stuck on the floor of the cage or the aviary), the lower abdominal region will appear a bit swollen and full of eggs.

When the female finch is finally ready to lay eggs, expect a clutch of eggs in a short while. Finches (even the smaller species) can lay up to ten eggs, though the average is three to six individual eggs per laying.

Do not be upset if the female finch does not appear interested in her first few eggs. Active incubation of the eggs will only happen once the *entire clutch* of the finch's eggs has appeared. So if a bird is not incubating a clutch of two eggs that means there are more coming!

What about hatching? Finch eggs usually hatch within *10 days* of active incubation. If you have a pair of very responsible finches, the incubation period will be handled well and all fertilized eggs *will* hatch. If the eggs did not hatch within the initial 10-day period, wait another six days.

If no chicks emerge, let's give your birds the benefit of the doubt. Wait another four days and check the nest again. If the eggs still have not responded to the incubation, these eggs will probably not hatch anymore. Better remove them from the nest, as unfertilized eggs will eventually rot and pollute the nest.

Notes on Finch Eggs

Some years ago, a myth emerged from the avian woodwork that finch eggs are fertilized by the males *after* the female finch has laid the eggs.

This is not true and will never be true because finches need to fertilize the eggs while still *inside* the body of the "hen", or female finch. Like other bird eggs, finch eggs are covered by hard, semi-porous shells that protect the developing embryo from the external environment.

But compared to other avian eggs, *finch eggs* are perhaps the most sensitive of all. Jarring dips in temperature and even a partially incomplete incubating period can prevent the embryo inside the egg from surviving.

If you need to handle the eggs, it's be best to wash your hands thoroughly with soap to remove most of the skin's natural oil (as this can block the porous material of the shell, which can kill the embryo) or you can just wear a pair of latex gloves. It is not true that once the birds get a whiff of your scent that they will abandon their eggs.

Finches abandon their eggs for the following reasons:

1. The eggs are not fertile.

2. This is the first time that the pair has mated and laid eggs. The female finch is still inexperienced.

3. The birds have yet to begin their egg-rearing duties.

It is possible for female finches to lay eggs even without males inside the aviary. But without males of course, all these eggs will not hatch. When a clutch of eggs goes "bad", female finches usually lay another clutch of eggs. If you have a strong, healthy pair, this won't be a problem at all.

Now, if you see your birds *tossing* the eggs away from the nest, simply put the eggs back in the nest and wait for a few days. If the birds still haven't started their egg-rearing activities, it would be best to transfer the eggs to another nest (this is called fostering) if you have another active pair in the aviary.

Either this or you can place the eggs in a box with warm bedding. Use a regular light bulb to warm the egg. It is a long shot, but it is still possible that you have fertile eggs and these eggs are just waiting for the mother to take care of them.

If you want to check if the eggs are alive, use the candle method. "Candling" is simply holding up the eggs to see the contents with the help of a strong light. Do this examination in a dark room so the contents of the avian eggs will be easier to see.

Just shine a light on the shell. If you see veins (these are usually pulsing "blobs" inside the egg), you have a live egg. Return the eggs in the exact same position that you found them. Avoid jarring the eggs and *don't crack* any of them!

Step Four: Finch Chicks!

In less than half a month, all fertilized eggs will begin to hatch. This is a great time to observe the finches, as their rearing behavior will emerge. If you see some finch chicks on the floor of the cage, simply put them back in.

Don't worry – your pet finches will still take care of their young even if you've handle one or two chicks. Unlike wild finches, the abandonment rate of captive finches is much lower because they are somewhat used to seeing humans near their home.

If the first group of chicks dies or only a few survive, don't fret. Your finches will breed again in the future (some breed all year long). Seasoned finch keepers don't like the idea of taking the chicks to manually warm and feed them.

The finches will not learn what they should do, and their natural rearing instincts will not fully emerge if they do not experience the hardship of raising a new family. Sad as it may seem, you really must allow

Mother Nature to teach your finches a thing or two about rearing a new family.

Common Finch Disorders & Diseases

Sad as it may seem, we have to be prepared for the first trip to the veterinarian. The first step in the healing process is always recognizing the problem. The following table contains the most common signs that a finch may be ill:

Area	Signs
Respiratory tract	The finch may be coughing or producing excessive amounts of mucus. The sinus region may also appear inflamed and almost always pasty. Some amount of crusting may also appear near the bird's eyes. If the bird is visibly struggling to breathe, then you are probably dealing with a respiratory anomaly.

Digestive process	The first thing to look for is irregularities in the stool or droppings of the finch. Regular droppings are a mix of dry waste and moisture. Sick birds will produce very watery stool with very foul odors. Infections in the digestive process also results in accelerated weight loss, which can be fatal to birds.
Reproductive system	Birds are unable to produce fertilized eggs. Females may be unable to expel the eggs.
Neurological problems	Any odd, repetitive behavior may signal neurological impairment.
General physical problems	Messy feathers or balding may occur. Cysts and tumors may also manifest.
General behavior	When a bird ceases from

	its regular activities (e.g. singing and preening), the bird is probably very ill.

There are literally hundreds of avian diseases that can affect finches in captivity. The following table lists only the most common illnesses so you can recognize the symptoms. As long as you can bring your pet finch to the veterinarian, there is a big chance of recovery from nearly all forms of avian diseases.

Disease	Description
Air sac mite	The finch may become very sluggish and inactive. Breathing may be labored and irregular. This disease occurs when tiny bird mites are able to penetrate the respiratory tract of the finch and stays in the small air sacs inside the finch's lungs.
Scaly face	Also cause by a species of bird mites, the face of the bird becomes very scaly and the skin becomes inflamed and may become infected.

Lice	Some species of mites prefer nesting on the skin and feathers of finches. Without proper treatment, lice infections can spread to other birds in the cage or aviary.
Intestinal parasites	Weight loss and watery droppings are a clear sign that something is up with the finch's digestive process. Without proper treatment, a whole flock can be decimated by intestinal parasites.
Egg-binding	The female finch is unable to move and her wings appear to be stiff and outstretched for no reason. Lower abdomen is usually distended. Treatment is surgical removal of the bound eggs.

Poor digestion and diarrhea	Reducing the amount of fresh food for a few days may help quell diarrhea. If this does not help, consult a veterinarian as diarrhea may be just a symptom of an underlying disease.
Star gazing	The bird may appear dizzy and off-balance. The head will most likely move from one side to another for no apparent reason. In the advanced stage of this disease, the bird will no longer be able to fly from one spot to another. Feeding and drinking becomes impossible. There is no known treatment for star gazing disorder.
Gastric yeast	Diarrhea and weight loss occurs. Stress inside the aviary or cage is the leading cause of gastric

	yeast, along with bad food choices.
	Probiotic supplementation and symptom treatment is a must. Finches can develop a natural immunity against gastric yeast problems over time.

References

Books:

Koepff, Christian & Romagano, **April *The Finch Handbook*** (New York: Barron's Educational Series, Inc.) 2001

Soucek, Gayle ***Gouldian Finches*** (New York: Barron's Educational Series, Inc.) 2000

Vriends, Matthew ***Gouldian Finches: A Complete Pet Owner's Manual*** (New York: Barron's Educational Series, Inc.) 1991

Website Resources

The Advantage of Small Specialist Breeding Flights
http://www.finchsociety.org/cfa/general/internals.htm
Air Sac Mites
http://www.finchniche.com/a-airsacmites.php
Avian Gastric Yeast (aka Megabacteria)
http://www.finchniche.com/a-agy.php
Bacterial Infection

http://www.finchniche.com/a-bacteria.php

Breeding Finches

http://www.finchandfinches.com/

Breeding or Life Routine?

http://www.ladygouldianfinch.com/features_breeding1.mgi

Building an Aviary

http://www.finchniche.com/a-aviary.php

Cage Bird Lighting

http://www.ladygouldianfinch.com/features_lighting.mgi

Cage or Aviary?

http://www.finchniche.com/a-cageaviary.php

Candling the Egg

http://www.finchniche.com/a-candling.php

Chick Development

http://www.finchniche.com/a-chickdevelopment.php

Chick Tossing & Nest Abandonment

http://www.finchniche.com/a-abandoned.php

Common Breeding Problems

http://www.finchniche.com/a-bproblems.php

Creating and Enjoying an Aviary

http://www.birdsnways.com/wisdom/ww26eii.htm

Eggs

http://www.finchniche.com/a-eggs.php

Fighting or Co-Exisiting

http://www.finchniche.com/a-fighting.php

Finch Behavior

http://www.finchniche.com/a-behavior.php

Finch Diets or a Mug's Guide to All Things Avian Edible

http://www.finchsociety.org/cfa/diet/diet.htm

Finch Food

http://www.finchniche.com/a-finchfood.php

Finches for Beginners or Welcome to the Club!!!!

http://www.finchsociety.org/cfa/general/begin/begin.htm

Finch Grasses

http://www.finchsociety.org/fsa/grass/grass.htm

Pair Bonding

http://www.finchniche.com/a-pairbond.php

A Sick Finch - Symptoms/Treatment

http://www.finchniche.com/a-sick.php

So You're Going to Breed Finches Then!!

http://www.finchsociety.org/cfa/nests/nests.htm

Twirling or Stargazing

http://www.finchniche.com/a-twirling.php

Visually Sexing Finches

http://www.finchniche.com/a-visuallysexing.php

Brevia Publishing Company
Schererville, Indiana